Our World

Rocks and soil

Neil Morris

Belitha Press

First published in the UK in 2002 by
Belitha Press
an imprint of Chrysalis Books plc
64 Brewery Road, London N7 9NT

Copyright © Belitha Press Ltd 2002
Text by Neil Morris

ISBN 1-84138-414-3

British Library Cataloguing in Publication Data
for this book is available from the British Library.

Series editor: Jean Coppendale
Designer: Peter Clayman
Artwork: Chris Forsey
Picture researchers: Terry Forshaw, Louise Daubeny, Jenny Barlow and Ashley
Brent
Consultant: Bethan Currenti

Printed in Hong Kong

10 9 8 7 6 5 4 3 2 1

Picture acknowledgements:
(T) = Top, (B) = Bottom, (L) = Left, (R) = Right.
C = Corbis, CI = Chrysalis Images, DV = Digital Vision, E = Ecoscene, FLPA = Frank Lane Picture Agency, GI
= Getty Images, P = Papilio, SP = Still Pictures, SPL = Science Photo Library.
Front cover (main) & 10 CI; Title Page, 7 & back cover (R) DV; 4 & front cover (inset) DV; 5 & back cover
(L) CI; 6 DV; 8 (T) Maurice Nimmo/FLPA, (B) Martin Land/SPL; 9 Sam Ogden/SPL; 11 (T) & front cover
(inset) Galen Rowell/C, (B) CI; 12 (T) CI, (B) & front cover (inset) FLPA/C; 13 & 31 (TR) CI; 14 (T) Erik
Schaffer/E, (B) Peter Frischmuth/SP; 15 GI/Jeremy Hardie; 16 Jecko Vassilev/SP; 17 (T) Vanni Archive/C,
(B) Jorgen Schytte/SP; 18 Gryniewicz/E; 19 & front cover (inset) Patrick Johns/C; 21 Gary Braasch/C; 22
B. Stein/SP; 23 (T) Robert Pickett/C, (B) Chris Demetrion/FLPA; 24 (T) Robert Pickett/P, (B) Pat O'Hara/C;
25 P/C; 26 & 31 (TL) Pierre Gleizes/SP; 27 (T) Nik Wheeler/C, (B) Mark Edwards/SP.

Contents

Our rocky Earth

We live on a planet called Earth. Our planet is round, like a football. The ground beneath our feet is the surface of the planet's outer layer. This layer, called the Earth's **crust**, is a bit like the peel around an orange.

This is how planet Earth looks from space.

Unlike orange peel, Earth's crust is hard. This is because it is made up entirely of rocks. Sometimes you can see the bare rocks clearly on mountains or cliffs.

These high mountain peaks show just how rocky our planet is.

Deep under ground

Further down under ground, below the Earth's crust, is a much thicker layer called the **mantle**. The rocks in the mantle are so hot that many of them have melted.

A volcano throws up a fountain of fiery sparks from deep under ground.

A river of hot rock, called lava, flows downhill from the top of a volcano.

The Earth's crust is cracked into huge pieces, called **plates**, like a giant jigsaw. The plates move slowly on top of the hot mantle. Sometimes **molten** rock moves up through cracks in the Earth's crust, making a spectacular **volcano**.

Minerals

The Earth's rocks are made of solid substances called **minerals**. There are thousands of different minerals, but only about a hundred of them are very common.

Some rocks, like this piece of granite, have many different minerals in them.

Amethyst is a precious stone made up of a mineral called quartz.

Some minerals have regular, even shapes. We call these **crystals**. Most of them form when heat deep inside the Earth melts the minerals in rocks.

Diamond is the hardest of all minerals. It is used as a jewel because it sparkles so brilliantly.

Then the minerals cool and harden into smooth-sided crystals.

Wearing away

The rocks that we see on the surface of the Earth face different weather all the time. Over many years the rocks get worn away and break down into smaller **particles**.

Caves are formed as water wears away softer kinds of rock.

Glaciers are like rivers of ice. They creep down mountains, carving out deep valleys.

Rock particles are often loosened by rainwater and carried away by rivers. Tiny particles may simply be blown away by the wind.

Rocks are worn away by wind and rain to make fantastic shapes.

Fossils

Fossils are the remains of animals and plants that lived millions of years ago. They keep their shape in rocks. Fossils are very useful to us, because they teach us about the history of life on Earth.

This fossil shows the spiral shape of shellfish that lived millions of years ago.

These plant fossils show the delicate details of fern leaves.

Everything we know about dinosaurs comes from finding fossils like these.

Many of the fossils that we find today show us kinds of animals that are no longer alive. No person has ever seen a live dinosaur, but we know what they looked like because of fossils.

Digging deep

Did you know that most of the energy we use to heat our homes and drive our cars comes from fossils? Coal, oil and gas were all formed from the remains of prehistoric plants and tiny animals. We call them **fossil fuels**.

This man is cutting **peat**, which is made of dead plant matter.

Buried peat turns into coal, which we mine for fuel.

Workers drill down into the seabed to find valuable oil.

We dig mines deep in the ground to find layers of coal. To get oil and natural gas, powerful drills go down a long way into the seabed. The oil and gas then flow through pipes to the surface.

Useful materials

We also get metals such as copper and tin from under the ground. They are found in special rocks called **ores**. Most ores have to be heated to get the metal out. One of the most **precious metals**, gold, is sometimes found in between rock layers.

This huge open mine is used for digging out copper.

Other rocks, such as **granite** and **marble**, are useful for building and making things. They are dug out in **quarries**. We also use clay and mud to make bricks and tiles.

White marble can be carved to make beautiful sculptures.

Once they have been shaped, mud bricks are left out in the sun to dry.

What is soil?

Soil is a layer of material that covers the ground. You can see lots of soil in gardens and in farmers' fields. All soil starts off as tiny pieces of rock that have been broken down over many years.

Farmers plough their fields before they plant seeds. The plough cuts into the soil, turning it over and breaking it up.

It takes even longer for the remains of rotting plants and animals to mix with rock fragments and minerals. When they do, the mixture makes soil.

Dead leaves fall to the forest floor, where they slowly rot away. This helps to make new soil.

Layers of soil

Soil is made up of different layers. At the surface is a thin layer of rotting leaves and other things that were once alive, such as insects. Over time these form a dark mass called **humus**.

This slice through soil shows its different layers:
1 humus
2 topsoil
3 subsoil
4 rock fragments
5 solid rock

Beneath this surface layer is **topsoil**, which is rich in humus. Below that is a layer of subsoil, which is full of minerals washed down from above. Deeper still, a layer of rock fragments lies on top of solid rock.

A tree's long roots often reach right down into the subsoil.

21

Improving soil

Soil makes an ideal home for many living things. Some, such as moles, are rarely seen above ground. They burrow away, breaking up the soil as they dig their long tunnels.

The mole has strong claws, which it uses like shovels to dig through the soil.

Earthworms stay underground most of the time, but come up to find plant matter.

Most underground animals are much smaller creatures, such as earthworms, beetles and ants. They also improve soil by breaking it up and mixing it as they move and eat.

The tiny tunnels made by ants and other insects let air and water into the soil.

Plant life

Plants are held in the soil by their **roots**, which they use to take in water and minerals. The roots are very useful to the soil. They help to stop it being blown or washed away in storms.

A plant's roots act like an anchor in the soil.

Small plants called lichens help to break rocks down and make soil.

In the mountains, some flowers even grow in cracks between rocks.

Large tree roots can help to break down rocks to make more soil. And when plants die, their roots, stems and leaves make the soil even richer.

Farming the land

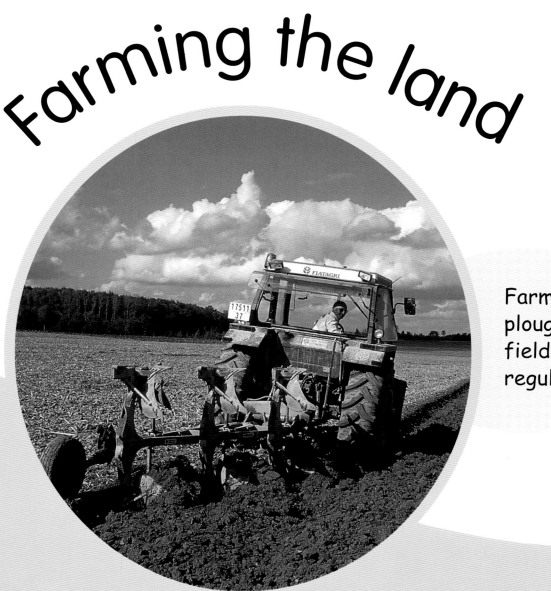

Farmers plough their fields regularly.

All farmers want to look after the soil in their fields. Sometimes they use chemicals to make their soil richer, but this can be harmful, especially to the water beneath the soil and rocks.

Some farmers protect their land by using **organic** methods to grow their crops. These farmers do not put chemicals on the soil to make their crops grow.

Sprays that kill insects and other pests can be harmful to soil and water.

Flat terraces help to stop soil being washed away by heavy rain.

Do it yourself

Find out how worms live and move in the soil.

Make your own wormery

1 Take a large plastic or glass jar and fill it three-quarters full with alternate layers of sand, gardener's compost and ordinary garden soil. Put the garden soil through a sieve first, to make it crumbly. Make each layer 2 or 3 cm deep, and water it before adding the next layer.

2 Put about 6 earthworms on top of the soil and cover them with dead leaves.

3 Cover the whole jar with a dark cloth (earthworms don't like the light, and this will give the wormery an underground effect).

4 When you take the cloth off, you'll see how the worms tunnel through the soil.

When you've finished with your wormery, don't forget to put all the worms back where you found them.

Glossary

crust The hard outer layer of the Earth.

crystals Solid forms of minerals, such as quartz, with regular, even shapes.

fossils The preserved remains of prehistoric animals and plants.

fossil fuels Fuels such as coal, oil or gas that have been made from the remains of living things.

glaciers Vast masses of ice that move very slowly down a mountain.

granite A hard rock that is widely used for building.

humus The dark mass of rotting plant and animal remains in soil.

mantle The thick layer of hot rock beneath the Earth's crust.

marble A white rock that is often used to carve statues.

minerals Solid chemical substances that occur naturally in the Earth's crust.

molten Describing something that has melted or turned into a liquid.

ores Rocks or minerals that contain useful metals.

organic Living or once living; also describes farming methods that use no chemicals such as artificial fertilizers or pesticides on the soil.

particles Tiny amounts of rock that may be as small as a speck of dust.

peat Underground matter made of dead plants that looks like dark, rich soil.

plates Pieces of the Earth's crust; the Earth's plates fit together like a giant jigsaw.

precious metals Valuable metals such as gold or silver.

quarries Places where rocks are dug out of the ground.

roots Parts of a plant that grow down into the soil and take in water and food.

topsoil An upper layer of soil.

volcano An opening through which molten (liquid) rock bursts out from deep inside the Earth; volcanoes often form mountains.

index